EARLY LEARNING EXPERIENCES IN LANGUAGE AND READING READINESS

by Imogene Forte and Joy MacKenzie

Incentive Publications, Inc.
Nashville, Tennessee

Illustrated by Gayle Seaberg Harvey
Cover Design by Marta Drayton
Edited by Leslie Britt

ISBN 0-86530-296-0

PRINTED IN THE UNITED STATES OF AMERICA

Table Of Contents

About This Book . . .

Early Learning Experiences in Language and Reading Readiness has been planned to help young children learn through experimentation, through creative involvement in directed activities, and finally, through the joy of discovery.

Young children are curious about and extremely sensitive to their environment. They instinctively push and pull, take apart and attempt to put together again, smell, taste, feel, and listen to things around them. "Why?" "What?" "When?" "Where?" and "How?" are words they use naturally and often. It is this interaction with their environment that parents and teachers can either nurture and encourage or inhibit and retard. Children who have had many happy, satisfying opportunities to use their hands, feet, eyes, ears, and whole bodies are much more apt to adjust happily and successfully to more structured language and reading experiences.

The purpose of the activities in *Early Learning Experiences in Language and Reading Readiness* is to help children learn to view reading as a method of communication and to appreciate and make creative use of language in everyday life.

The book includes a mix of high-interest directed pencil-and-paper activities, discussion, and open-ended creative activities. While instructions are directed to the child, an adult will, of course, need to read and interact with the child in the interpretation and completion of the activities. Ideally, the projects will be presented in a stress-free setting that will afford time for the child to question, wonder, and ponder—and to develop an abiding, imaginatively inquisitive approach to developing language and reading skills and concepts. Each activity is intended to contribute to the development of a sound foundation upon which the basic skills necessary for school readiness may be built. They have also been planned to provide a flexibility and freedom to enhance the child's growth in social interaction and creative self-expression.

Which is the way to Wednesday?
Is it up or down?
This way, that way, forward, backward —
Should I turn around?

They say the way is easy,
It won't be hard to know
If I can read the signposts
That tell me where to go . . .

Each symbol, word and picture
Will help me find my way,
So I will read them carefully
To see just what they say!

YOU CAN READ FACES!

Think of a word that tells about the feeling each face is showing.
Can you make your face show the same word?

Look at the faces of the people on this street.
Point to a happy face, a sad face, an angry face, an excited face.

YOU CAN READ SIGNALS!

Can you tell what the person in each picture is saying?

Can you think of another way to signal . . .

. . . for help?

. . . for love?

. . . for an invitation?

YOU CAN READ SIGNS AND SYMBOLS!

As you touch each picture, tell about its message.

ALL AROUND THE TOWN

This town is filled with all kinds of signs.
How many of them can you read?

Just for fun, add some signs of your own to this picture.

My Name Is _____

13

YOU CAN READ PICTURES!

Read the picture stories. Which one has a happy ending? Which one shows how you and your friends would act?

Everyone likes a story with a happy ending!

A PICTURE POEM . . . ABOUT LOVE

I ♥ (ice cream)
I ♥ (pies)
I ♥ (kittens)
And (butterflies)
I ♥ (bubbles)
I ♥ (kites)
I ♥ (rainbows)
And (starry nights)

What part of the poem do you like best?
Find the words in the poem that rhyme.
Circle them!

Can you finish this part of the poem
by supplying the last word?

I like lots of things you see,
But most of all, I like _____!

You might try writing a picture poem of your very own!
Make it tell about the things you love.

My Name Is _____

YOU CAN READ NUMBERS!

What do the numbers on this page tell?
Can you think of another place you might go
where there are lots of numbers to read?

GET GUS GUGGLEWUMP'S NUMBER!

Ask a grownup to help you use a large piece of paper
to do a rubbing of the license plate on a car.

Hold your rubbing next to the license plate
on Gus Gugglewump's car.
Color the numbers on your rubbing that are the same as
the numbers on Gus's license plate.

YOU CAN READ LETTERS!

Touch each letter in this picture and say its name.
Did you find all 26 letters of the alphabet? Color them.

My Name Is _____

18

DOT-TO-DOT, FROM A TO Z

Draw dot-to-dot
From A to Z,
And a funny animal
You will see!

E

G   F   D   Z

Y

C

H

B

O   A

N

S   T

P

U

V

I

J   L

M   Q   R   W   X

K

Color the animal and give it a name.

My Name Is _____

YOU CAN READ WORDS!

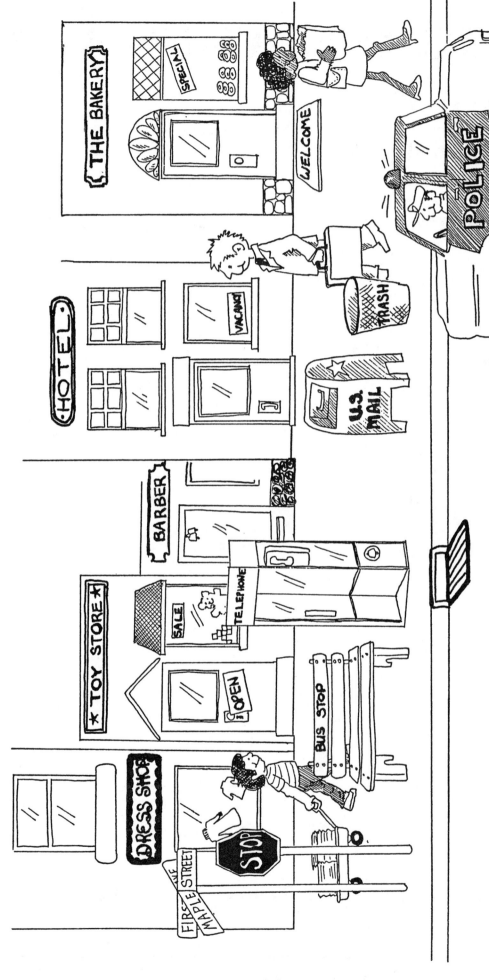

When you walk on a sidewalk in a town or city, you see many signs. Words are everywhere! How many of these words can you read?

THE WORD CONNECTION

Draw a line from each word to the object or objects it describes.
(Some will have more than one answer!)

sweet

rough

prickly

cold

bright

lovely

salty

wiggly

soft

sour

warm

slippery

Draw some additional pictures that fit these words!

My Name Is _____

CEREAL BOX SPECIAL

Make yourself a bowl of cereal.
As you eat the cereal, try to read the words on the cereal box.

Can you find

   . . . a word that begins with P?

   . . . a word that has four letters?

   . . . a word that ends in E?

   . . . a word that has a soft sound?

   . . . a word that is fun to hear?

Try to think of a word that can tell someone

   . . . how the cereal looks.

     . . . how the cereal feels on your tongue.

      . . . how the cereal smells.

       . . . how the cereal sounds.

        . . . how the cereal tastes.

22

MIX AND MATCH

You can make a game to match words with pictures!

Cut out all (36) of the picture and word cards on these pages.
Have someone read the word cards and look over
the picture cards with you.

Mix up all of the cards and spread them out on the floor
or on a table. Ask a friend to help you match the words
with the correct picture.

You can even enjoy this game all by yourself!

ball	cup	shoe
tree	duck	cat

24   © 1995 by Incentive Publications, Inc., Nashville, TN.

boy	penny	fork
flower	book	moon
pencil	sun	girl
apple	box	bear

ALPHABET BOX

Collect something that begins
with each letter of
the alphabet.

Mark each item with its
beginning letter.

Make a special box.
Cover the outside with ABCs
of all sizes and colors.
Put all your ABC items
in the box.

See if you can make up a game using your ABC objects.

PICTURES TELL THE STORY

Can you read the story these pictures tell?
Share your story with someone and color the pictures.

My Name Is _____

Read the story these pictures tell.
Draw one more picture to finish the story.

1.

2.

3.

Show your completed story to someone else.
See if they can read it back to you!

My Name Is _____

IT'S A CIRCUS!

The circus has come to town, and it's time for the animals
to take their places in the BIG TOP show ring!
Color and cut out the animals.
Then paste each one in its proper place in the show ring.

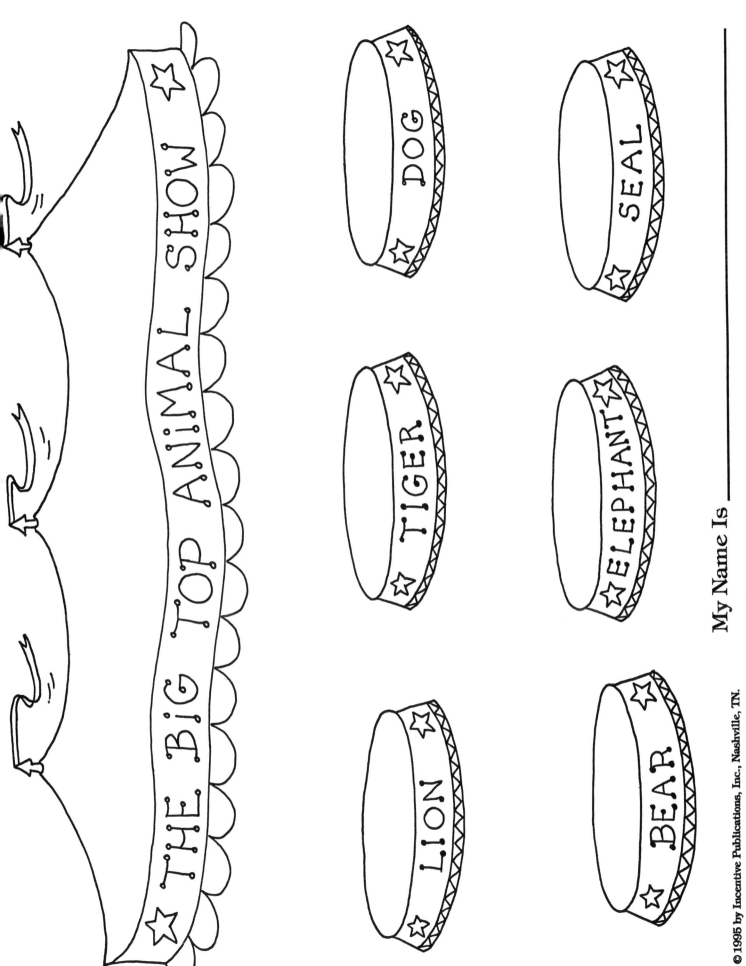

THE BiG TOP ANiMAL SHOW

DOG

SEAL

TIGER

ELEPHANT

LION

BEAR

My Name Is _____

LETTER TRAIN

Supply the letters that are missing on each car of the ABC Circus Train.
Be sure that every car has a capital letter and a lower-case letter.

My Name Is _____

My Name Is _____

33

BALANCING ACT

Cut out the seals and balls along the dotted lines.
Each seal should be balancing balls
that show words beginning with
the same letter as the one on his stand.

alligator

cat

apple

airplane

clown

comb

cup

bird

ant

bee

book

butterfly

A

B

C

My Name Is _____

DINOSAUR MATCH

In each row, color *only* the two dinosaurs that are exactly alike.

Draw two dinosaurs of your own that look as nearly alike
as you can make them.

My Name Is _____

A DAY AT THE FARM

Finish the farm scene.
Draw yourself on the farm
doing something you would like to do.

My Name Is _____

PIGS ON THE PATH

Draw a picture to show what you think will happen next!

My Name Is _____

IT'S ABOUT TIME!

Cut out the clock face and the hands.
Paste the face on a small paper plate.
Use a paper fastener to attach the hands at the dot on the nose!

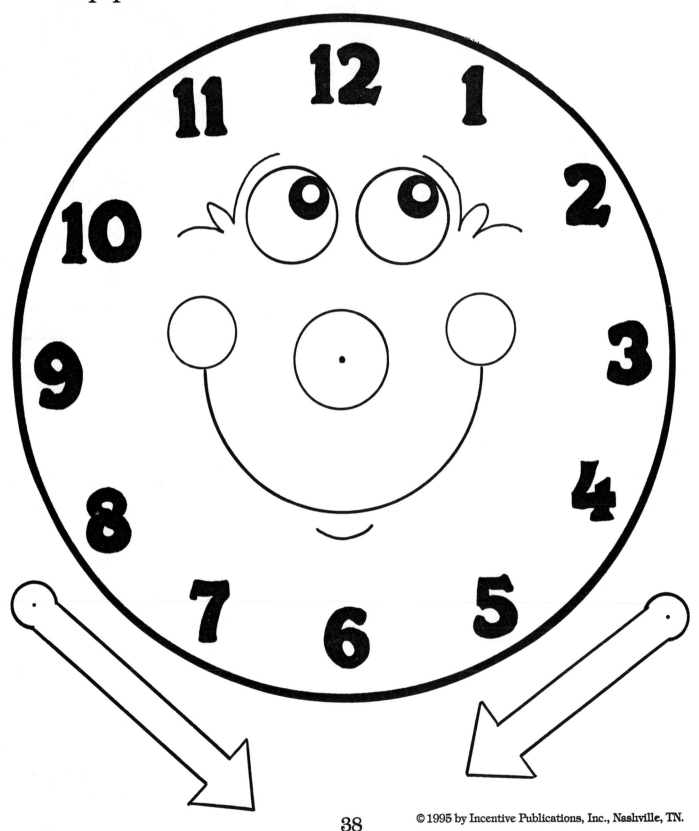

Now cut on the dotted lines to make a stack of word cards.
Shuffle the cards and stack them face down.
As you pick each card, read the time word and
move the hands on the clock face to show the correct time.

one	two	three
four	five	six
seven	eight	nine
ten	eleven	twelve

A FOREST PICNIC

These animals are getting ready to go on a picnic.
Count the animals in each family
to help them find their proper places.

POSITIVELY
NO
HUNTING

Look at the picnic picture below.
Count the number of plates to see
where the families need to sit.

Can you show the animal families
to their tables?

ANTS MUST
STAY AT THEIR
OWN TABLES!

My Name Is _____

TOUCH AND TELL

Words can tell us how things feel when we touch them.
Try touching some of the things on the list below.
See how many words you can think of that describe how each one feels.

Ask someone to write the words on a long strip of paper so that you can put it on the wall in your room.

- Water against your hand

- A pillow under your head

- A powder puff against your cheek

- Bubbles all around you in the tub

- Hair or an animal's fur

- Ear lobes

- A horse's nose

- Mud or sand between your toes

- Your nose in Teddy Bear's neck

- Shaving cream on your face

- Pinching marshmallows

- Chocolate pudding on your tongue

- Gelatin squished in your hand

Do you have other favorite things to touch? How do they feel?

NO FAIR PEEKING!

Look carefully at the picture.
Now cover the picture.
Draw the picture as you remember it on another sheet of paper.

Compare the two pictures to see how well you remembered.

My Name Is _____

43

MATCH-UP

In each line, color only the pictures that go together.
Make an X on the picture that does not belong.

My Name Is _____

ACT OUT A RHYME

Ask someone to read the rhymes aloud to you.
Listen carefully, then act out each rhyme.

HOW TO SHAKE HANDS WITH AN OCTOPUS

Pleased to meet you,   *(hands on hips)*
How-do-you-do?   *(salute)*
I want to shake hands,
But I have only two!   *(hold out two hands)*
How shall we manage?   *(draw big question*
I would hate   *mark in the air)*
To miss even one
Of your friendly eight!

"Well," said Octopus,
"I have found
It's best to shake
As you walk around —   *(circle the octopus,*
Hand-over-hand,   *shaking each*
One-two-three-four,   *of its eight hands,*
Hand-over-hand,   *hand-over-hand)*
Five-six, then MORE!"

JUNGLE GYM

Climb up an elephant   *(climb)*
Slide down his trunk—Whee! *(slide)*
Swing on the tail   *(swing)*
Of a giant monkey.
Crawl up the neck   *(crawl)*
Of a tall giraffe,
Then tickle his belly   *(tickle)*
And make him laugh!

My Name Is _____

MAKE A KRISPY KRITTER!

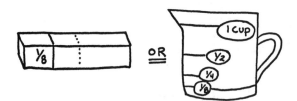

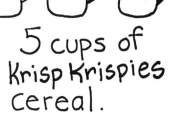

⭐ Melt ⅛ cup of margarine or butter.

⭐2 Mix with 4 cups of miniature marshmallows and 5 cups of Krisp Krispies cereal.

⭐3 Stir until cereal is coated.

⭐4 Wet hands with cold water and shape the mixture into all sorts of imaginary animals.

Mmm !

⭐5 Use raisins, nuts and candies for faces, spots and details.

ANIMAL SAFARI

Draw a mother animal with a baby.   Draw a long-necked animal.

Draw a large animal with a trunk.   Draw two birds in a tree.

Use yellow, brown, red and green crayons to color the animals.

My Name Is _____

PICTURE TALK

Draw a line from each picture to the word or phrase
that best describes it.
Color the pictures and make up a story to go with each one.

BAD NEWS

FUN IN THE SUN

AUTUMN

HAPPY BIRTHDAY

GOOD-BYE!

My Name Is _____

A STORY TO FINISH

Read the story below with a friend.

DOUBLE TROUBLE

Billy and Betty are neighbors and best friends.
They play together every day.
Today, Billy's dog chewed up Betty's favorite toy.

Now draw a picture to show what you think happened next.

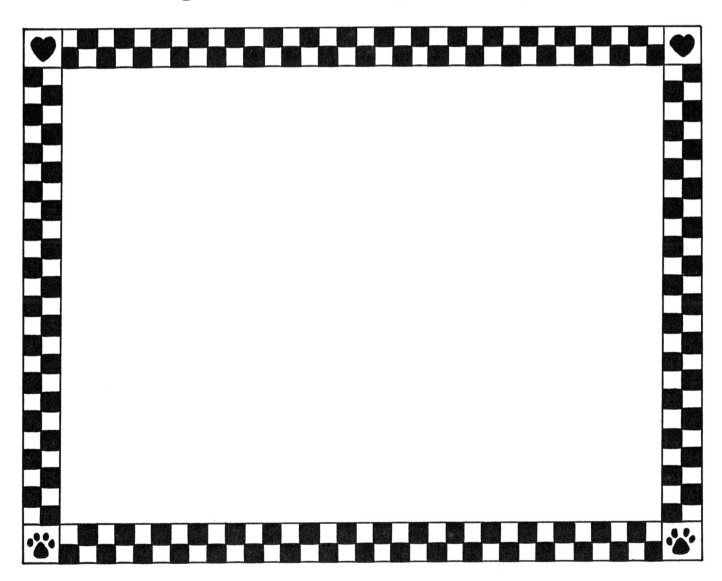

Do you think Billy and Betty will still be best friends?

My Name Is _____

LOOK-ALIKES

Sometimes a real-life object appears to have the shape of an alphabet letter.
Touch each picture and tell the name of a letter you see in the picture.
Write that letter on the line under the picture.

My Name Is _____

THE ALPHABET TREE

Color and cut out the tree.
Cut on the solid lines and fold on the dotted lines
to open the little "windows" in the tree.

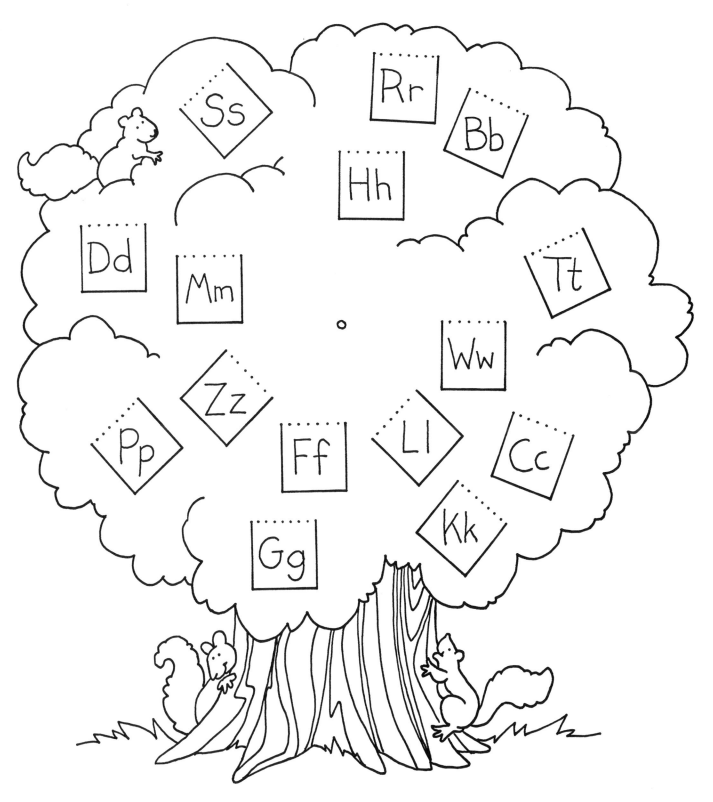

Color and cut out the picture wheel.
Punch a paper fastener through the hole in the center of the tree
to attach the wheel to the back of the tree.

Look at the alphabet letter on each window and turn the wheel
until a picture whose name begins with that letter
appears in the open space.

Try to find the right match for each letter.

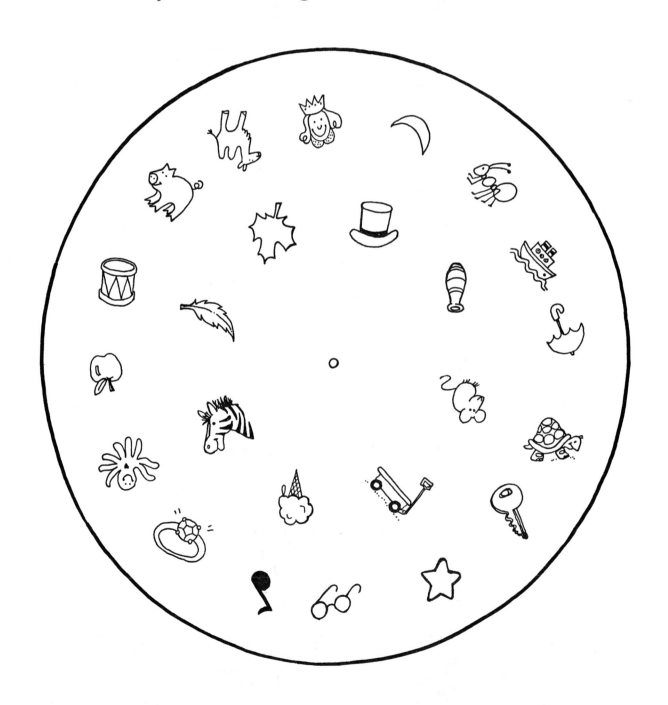

EASY AS A-B-C

Color all the pictures.
Then cut on the heavy lines to make your ABC cards.
See if you can lay them in order on the floor.

A a

B b

C c

D d

E e

F f

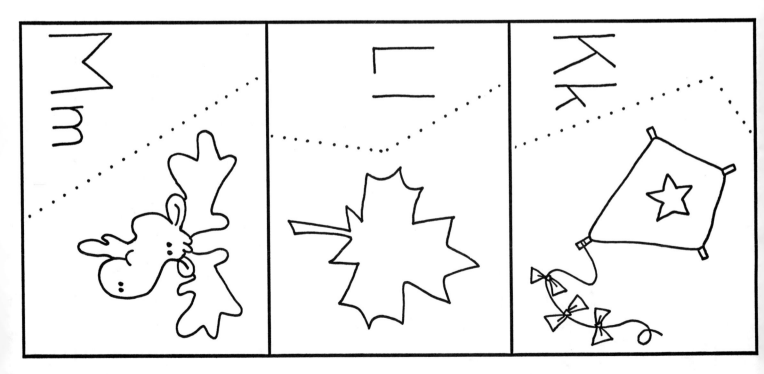

54

To play a matching game, cut on the dotted lines
to separate the letter from each card.
Now put them back together, matching the letters and pictures.

LETTER SETS

You will need some clip-on clothespins, tape, and scissors for this activity.
Cut out the letter wheels and the single letter cards below.
Tape each single letter to the top of a clothespin.
See if you can match the sets of lower-case and capital letters
by clipping each clothespin in the proper place on the wheel.

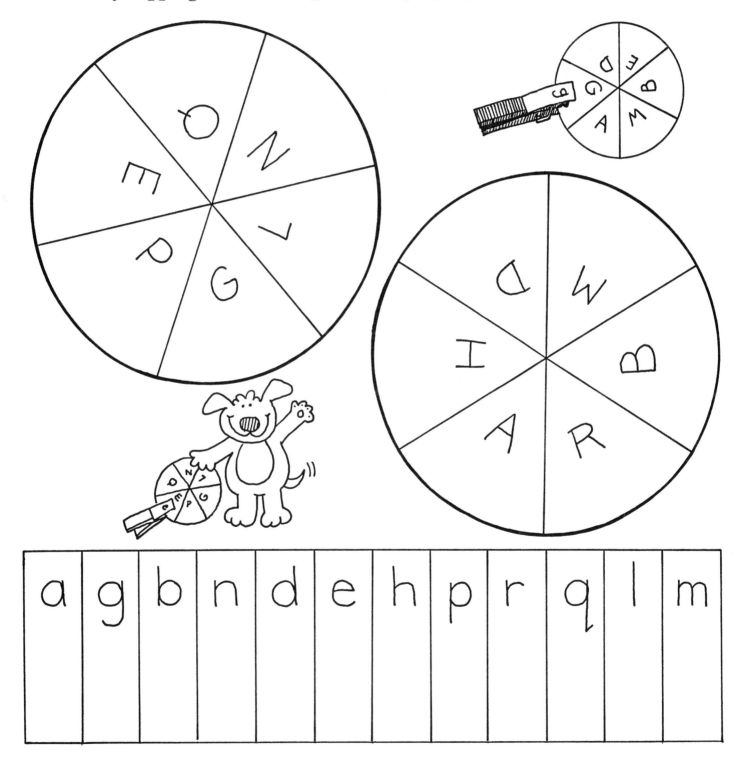

a	g	b	n	d	e	h	p	r	q	l	m

A BERRY HUNGRY BEAR!

This bear has had quite a busy day at the campground!

Look at the pictures in order and make up a story
that tells about his day.
Draw your own picture in the empty box
to show how his day probably ended.

My Name Is _____

TV TIME

Turn on your TV set to see how many different TV programs you can make up. Here's how! Paste the TV screen and picture strips below on a piece of heavy construction paper. Then cut out the picture strips and the TV.
Cut on the dotted lines to make slots in the TV screen.
Slip the two picture strips through the slots as shown.
Be sure that Strip A is on the left and Strip B is on the right. Move the strips so that any two pictures are "showing" on the TV screen.
Use the pictures to make a sentence that tells about the program.

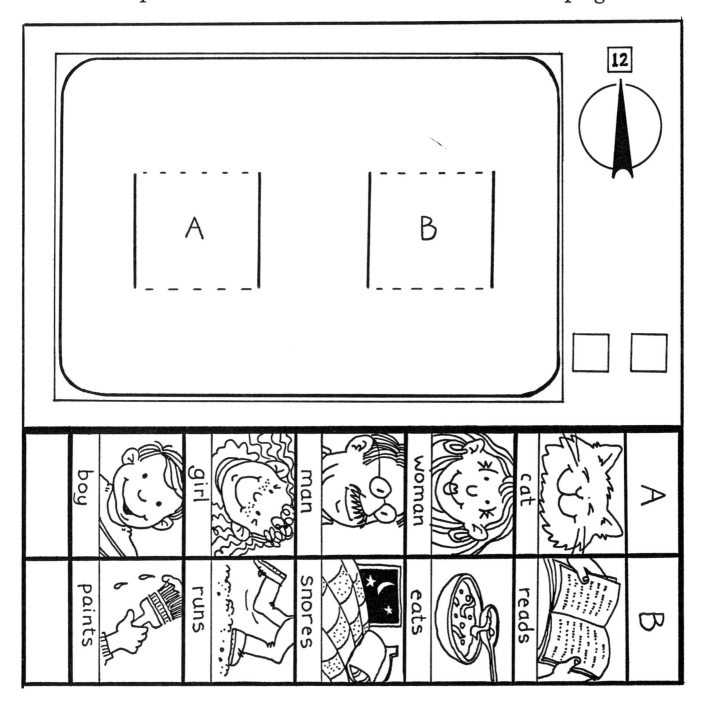

SILLY RHYMES

Listen to each rhyme. Use the pictures
to help you write the correct rhyming word in each space.

Can you tell who took my _____ ?

Oh I see. It was my _____ !

Can you guess who combs my _____ ?

Did you think it was a _____ ?

Who is swimming in my _____ ?

Did you see that funny _____ ?

Who is wearing my new _____ ?

Did you guess it was a _____ ?

My Name Is _____

CHARLIE'S PLACE

Choose your lunch from this menu.
Can you tell how much each item will cost?
Which of these foods is NOT sold here?

hamburger   waffle   hot dog

What can you buy for 25¢?
How many gum balls can you buy for a nickel?

My Name Is _____

MIXED-UP SIGNS

The words on these signs are mixed up.
Can you tell what the signs *should* say?

LOVE YOU I

SHUT DOOR THE PLEASE

FEED DON'T THE BEARS

Make up some words for the empty sign.
Ask someone to help you write your message.

My Name Is _____

BODY LANGUAGE

Look carefully at each circled picture.
Say its name aloud to yourself.
Then see if you can find a body part whose name rhymes with that picture.
Draw a line to connect the rhyming objects.

My Name Is _____

PICK A PET!

Read the poem with someone.

If you could pick an animal,
To take home as your pet,
Would you want the skunk,
Or the turtle, soaking wet?

Or would you choose the great big bear,
Who'd eat up all your honey?
How about the wise old wolf,
Who thinks the bear is funny?

HONEY

OLD BEARS
NEED LOTS
OF LOVE!

My Name Is _____

Maybe the horse could be your pet,
And take you for a ride.
Or the lion just might be more your style,
to lie down by your side.

It doesn't matter which you choose
To be your special friend,
Because even if your pet's not real,
It's fun to just pretend!

READ A RIDDLE

It is the name of a place.
It is full of wonderful things.
You may choose some things you would like to take home.
But it is not a store!
Can you name this place?

Use a different colored crayon to trace the path from each letter
to its correct box at the bottom.
Write the letters in the boxes and you will be able to see
the answer to the riddle.

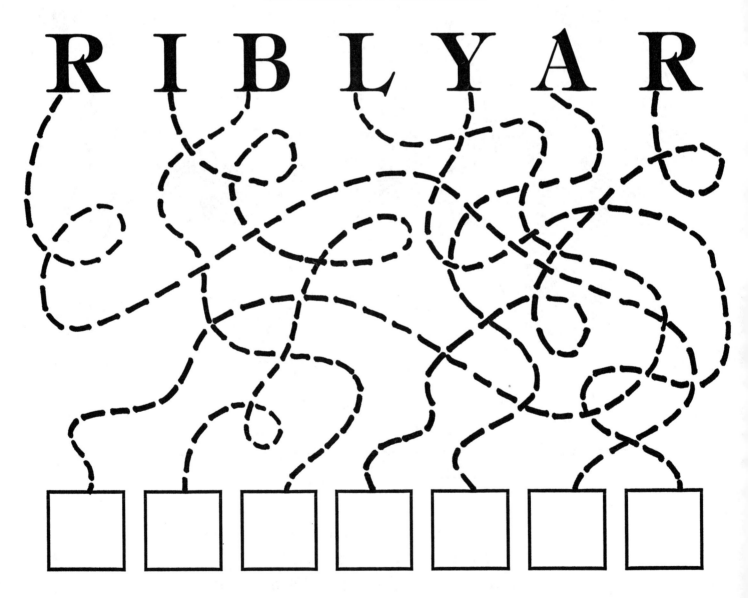

R I B L Y A R

My Name Is _____

THE WONDERFUL WORLD OF THE LIBRARY

Plan a trip to the library to get your very own library card.

The librarian will want to know . . .
- . . . your name.
- . . . your address.
- . . . your telephone number.
- . . . your parent's name.
- . . . your age.

Practice writing this information here:

NAME _____

ADDRESS _____

_____

AGE _____

PHONE_____

PARENT or GUARDIAN _____

LIBRARY LINGO

You will need to find out . . .
    . . . when the library is open.
    . . . how long you can keep books.
    . . . what the library rules are.
    . . . the name of a book you want to check out.

Ask a grownup to help you
write this information here.

My Name Is _____

CHOOSE A BOOK

Choose a favorite book.
Ask someone you like to read the book to you.

Ask the same person to write the name of the book here.

_____

Use this space to draw a picture that you think would make
a good cover for the book.

My Name Is _____

HOLD THAT PLACE!

Every reader needs a special reminder to mark his or her place in a book.

Find a piece of ribbon, lace, vinyl, or leather and cut it to mark your favorite page in a special book.

Cut a strip from colored construction paper and decorate it with felt-tip pens.

Cut a corner from an envelope and paste a pretty picture on it.

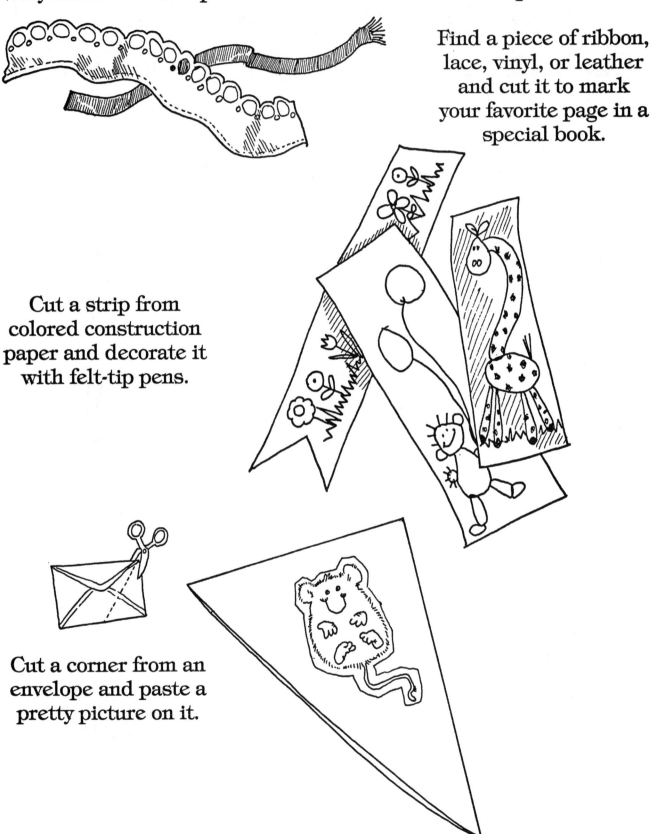

Write your whole name
on heavy white paper
and cut around it.

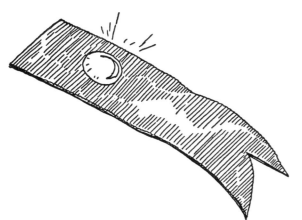

Glue a pretty bead
or a button
to a ribbon.

Twist some yarn
together to make
a tassel.

OR

Make several of these and give all but one to your friends!

WILLY WORM

Use a yellow wax crayon to color *only* the letters on Willy Worm.
Then use some tempera paint and a brush
to paint over Willy's whole body.

Cut on the dotted lines to make a
Willy Worm puzzle.

Now see if you can
paste Willy together
again on another
piece of paper.

If you want to keep Willy, cut him out and use him
for a bookmark!

YOUR VERY OWN
READING RECORD

On each book shape, write the name of a book you have read.
Then draw a picture on the nearby page to show something you
remember from the story.

My Name Is _____

Welcome to Wednesday!

Which is the way to Wednesday?
I've found it! I am here!
Each signpost told me what to do
The messages were clear.

Past Sunday, Monday, Tuesday,
To the middle of the week,
I walked down the road toward Happy,
Crossed the bridge at Giggle Creek.

And there I saw the welcome sign —
It's Wednesday! — Yes, indeed!
I can find my way to ANYWHERE
Since I know how to read!

TUESDAY

BEWARE!
MONDAY

"CHAMP"

WedNes-
Day
oR Bust!

Sunday

74

Teacher's Notes

QUICK AND EASY ACTIVITIES

The following quick and easy activities may be used to extend skills and concepts presented in *Early Learning Experiences in Language and Reading Readiness*.

- Put a child's name on a chair, on his or her place at a table or desk, on a bulletin board, and in as many other places in the room as possible. Remember, no other word is quite as special to the young child!

- Sing and enjoy "If You're Happy and You Know It, Clap Your Hands." Then try to "read" people's expressions in the group. Distribute the outlines of three faces to each child, and ask the children to make one face happy, one face sad, and one face surprised.

- Make construction paper traffic signals. Ask children to dictate language experience stories to show a signal used.

- Make a row of letters on the chalkboard. Include in the row two letters that are alike. Ask a child to find the two that are alike.

- Cut up comic strips for practice in sequencing events.

- Provide construction paper or oak tag, crayons, and scissors for children to use to design and cut out license plates (with numbers, of course!). Tape license plates to children's chairs, and ask other children to read the numerals during the day.

- Make construction paper flowers with different numbers of petals. Direct children to match those two having the same number of petals. (This is a good manipulative bulletin board or learning center activity that provides reinforcement of both numeral recognition and visual discrimination skills.)

- Enjoy "Alphabet Fishing." Print letters on fish shapes. Use a hula hoop for the pond. Ask children to fish out letters of your choosing.

- Sneak a little learning into Halloween fun with a "Spook House" bulletin board. Place alphabet letters along the path to a picture of a spooky house. Let children "walk" along the path with their fingers and say the letters. The first one to reach the house wins the game.

- Use the alphabet as a classroom management technique by saying the letters of the alphabet aloud. When a child hears the first letter of his or her first name, he or she goes to the library, retrieves his or her coat to go home, etc.

- Put small objects in baby food jars or other small glass jars. Print words on cards and place them in a learning center so that children may match objects with words.

- Print color words on sock shapes cut from white construction paper. Children may match with sock shapes cut from colored construction paper. For winter months, cut out mitten shapes, and for summer months cut out sneaker shapes.

- Write on the chalkboard a list of words that correspond with common classroom objects. Print the same words on large index cards. Ask children to match the word cards with the words on the board and then to locate the actual objects in the classroom.

- Make a "Parking Spaces" gameboard by drawing parking spaces on posterboard and printing alphabet letters in the spaces. To play the game, a child draws letter cards from a stack and "parks" them in the correct spaces.

- Make up two-line jingles and let children supply the rhyming words—the sillier, the better!

- Have children draw pictures of a topsy-turvy situation (at a picnic, at school, in a department store, etc.).

- Start an open-ended story about a family's topsy-turvy day. Go around the group, allowing children to add to and develop the story. Put the story on a chart and provide time for children to draw pictures to accompany it.

- Make several sets of construction paper hats—two alike and one slightly different. Let a child find the one that is different. (Hats could also be made from felt and used on a flannel board.)

- Ask each child to fold a sheet of drawing paper into four sections. Give explicit directions for drawing in each section, such as, "Draw something that makes you happy in the upper left-hand section; draw four flower pots in the lower right-hand section," etc.

- Label objects around the room, such as window, door, chair, table, and book, for vocabulary reinforcement.

- Make ice-cream cones of construction paper, and write color words on them. Have construction paper ice-cream scoops in different colors for matching.

- Make a "color worm" for each of the primary colors. Cut worms into puzzle parts (no more than three), and ask children to reassemble the worms to spell words.

- Play a game of "Follow the Directions." Give a child more than one direction to follow, such as, "Stand beside the easel, crawl under the table, and walk ten steps ahead." Increase difficulty as you think children are ready.

- Print the following instructions on a chart, and place it in a conspicuous place for children to read on their own.

Stop, look, and listen

Before you cross the _____

Use your _____

Use your _____

And then use your _____

- Cut from magazines advertisements of popular products that children will recognize. Ask children to match each product with its slogan, or use two copies of the advertisement for matching and for "reading" the name of the product.

- Print the names of the months of the year on a picture of a twelve-layer birthday cake. Print children's names and birth dates on flowers or some sort of decoration to be placed on the cake, and draw six candles at the top.

- Make simple hats or headbands, print the names of the months on them, and number them one through twelve. Let a child find his or her birthday month, put the months in order, etc.

- Make a collection of interesting pictures. Let a child choose one and dictate a story to an adult. Make the story and picture into a booklet. Or help the group of children write a story together. (See instructions for making your own book on the next page.)

Directions For Making Class Or Individual Booklets

1. Assemble all your materials:
   - Plain paper for pages
   - construction paper for cover
   - Scissors
   - Crayons or paint
   - Paper-hole puncher
   - Yarn or shoestring

2. Cut four or five large sheets of paper in half for either an eight-page or ten-page book.

3. Plan the contents of the book.

4. Work on one page at a time. Use crayons or paint to illustrate each page, or cut illustrations from old magazines and paste them on the page.

5. Arrange and number the pages.

6. Use construction paper or lightweight poster board to make a cover. Illustrate the cover any way you choose. (Be sure to add the author's name!)

7. Stack the pages of the book, place the cover on top, and punch four holes in the left edge of the stack with a paper-hole puncher. Tie the cover and pages together with a shoestring or a piece of sturdy yarn.
   - This same process may be used as a group project to produce one giant book for the classroom reading center or school library.

Read a good book every day! There is no better way to help young children develop a love for reading and an appreciation for good books. Don't forget to make time for your own reading—teachers count, too!

Here are some not-to-be-missed classics that all children will enjoy and remember!

Alexander and the Terrible, Horrible, No Good, Very Bad Day, by Judith Viorst. Atheneum, 1972.

And I Mean It, Stanley, by Crosby Newell Bonsall. Harper & Row, 1974.

Are You My Mother?, by P. D. Eastman. Random House, 1960.

Bedtime for Frances, by Russell Hoban. Harper, 1960.

Blueberries for Sal, by Robert McCloskey. Viking, 1948.

Brown Bear, Brown Bear, What Do You See?, by Bill Martin, Jr. Holt, 1983.

The Carrot Seed, by Ruth Krauss. Harper & Row, 1945.

The Cat in the Hat, by Dr. Seuss. Random House, 1957.

Chicken Soup with Rice, by Maurice Sendak. Harper, 1962.

A Color of His Own, by Leo Lionni. Pantheon, 1975.

Dinosaurs, by Gail Gibbons. Holiday, 1987.

Frederick, by Leo Lionni. Pantheon, 1967.

Gilberto and the Wind, by Marie Ets. Viking Press, 1963.

The Giving Tree, by Shel Silverstein. Harper, 1964.

Goodnight Moon, by Margaret Wise Brown. Harper, 1934.

Green Eggs and Ham, by Dr. Seuss. Random House, 1960.

Harold and the Purple Crayon, by Crockett Johnson. Harper, 1955.

Katy and the Big Snow, by Virginia Lee Burton. Houghton Mifflin, 1943.

The Little Engine That Could, by Watty Piper. Platt and Munk, 1961.

The Little House, by Virginia Lee Burton. Houghton Mifflin, 1939.

May I Bring a Friend?, by Beatrice de Regniers. Atheneum, 1964.

Mike Mulligan and His Steam Shovel, by Virginia Lee Burton. Houghton Mifflin, 1939.

Ming Lo Moves the Mountain, by Arnold Lobel. Greenwillow, 1982.

The Napping House, by Audrey Wood. Harcourt, 1984.

Noah's Ark, by Peter Spier. Doubleday, 1977.

Rain Makes Applesauce, by Julian Scheer and Marvin Bileck. Holiday, 1964.

Stand Back, Said the Elephant, I'm Going To Sneeze, by Patricia Thomas. Lothrop & Lee, 1971.

The Story about Ping, by Marjorie Flack. Viking Press, 1933.

Tikki Tikki Tembo, by Arlene Mosel. Holt, 1968.

Why Mosquitoes Buzz in People's Ears: A West African Tale, by Verna Aardema. Dial, 1975.